Rookie
Read-About®
Science

Remarkable
Reptiles

by Lisa M. Herrington

Content Consultant
Dr. Lucy Spelman
Zoological Medicine Specialist

Reading Consultant
Jeanne M. Clidas, Ph.D.
Reading Specialist

Children's Press®
An Imprint of Scholastic Inc.

Library of Congress Cataloging-in-Publication Data
Herrington, Lisa M., author.
Remarkable reptiles/by Lisa M. Herrington.
    pages cm. — (Rookie read about science. Strange animals)
Summary: "Introduces the reader to remarkable reptiles." — Provided by publisher.
Includes index.
ISBN 978-0-531-22603-2 (library binding) — ISBN 978-0-531-22749-7 (pbk.)
    1. Reptiles—Juvenile literature. I. Title.
QL644.2.H48 2016
    597.9—dc23   2015021146

Produced by Spooky Cheetah Press
Design by Keith Plechaty

© 2016 by Scholastic Inc.

Printed in China 62

SCHOLASTIC, CHILDREN'S PRESS, ROOKIE READ-ABOUT®, and associated logos
are trademarks and/or registered trademarks of Scholastic Inc.

1 2 3 4 5 6 7 8 9 10 R 25 24 23 22 21 20 19 18 17 16

Photographs: ©: cover: Rick Stevens/Fairfax Syndication; 3 top left: Baishev/
Shutterstock, Inc.; 3 top right: GlobalP/iStockphoto; 3 bottom: fivespots/Shutterstock,
Inc.; 4: Teguh Tirtaputra/Shutterstock, Inc.; 7: NHPA/Superstock, Inc.; 8: Animals
Animals/Superstock, Inc.; 11: Kim Taylor/Minden Pictures; 12 left: Minden Pictures/
Superstock, Inc.; 12 right: John Sullivan/Alamy Images; 15: NaturePL/Superstock, Inc.;
16: John Serrao/Science Source; 19 top: idp australia collection/Alamy Images; 19
bottom: Ryan M. Bolton/Shutterstock, Inc.; 20 top left: Fabio Liverani/Nature Picture
Library; 20 top right: Pete Oxford/Minden Pictures; 20 bottom left: reptiles4all/
Shutterstock, Inc.; 20 bottom right: Nature Picture Library/Alamy Images; 23 top
left, 23 top right, 23 bottom: Kim Taylor/Minden Pictures; 24: Nazzu/Shutterstock,
Inc.; 26 main: Jeremy Woodhouse/Media Bakery; 26 inset: Raymond Mendez/
Animals Animals; 27: Minden Pictures/Superstock, Inc.; 28 top: John Cancalosi/Alamy
Images; 28 bottom: Kevin Schafer/Alamy Images; 28-30 background: ImagePost/
Shutterstock, Inc.; 29 top: Gudkov Andrey/Shutterstock, Inc.; 29 center: Manfred
Gottschalk/Alamy Images; 29 bottom: A & J Visage/Alamy Images; 30: Ernst
Mutchnick/Alamy Images; 31 top: John Sullivan/Alamy Images; 31 center top: john
michael evan potter/Shutterstock, Inc.; 31 center bottom: Ian Cridlin/Thinkstock; 31
bottom: kajornyot/Shutterstock, Inc.

Table of Contents

That's Remarkable!

Reptiles are amazing animals. Alligators and snakes are reptiles. So are turtles. Some reptiles are stranger than you think!

The frilled lizard has a secret. If a **predator** comes close, it does something remarkable!

Surprise! The frilled lizard opens a flap of skin around its head. This makes the lizard look bigger and scarier. It opens its mouth and hisses.

FUN FACT!

The frilled lizard is known as the bicycle lizard. When it runs on its back legs, it looks like it is riding a bike!

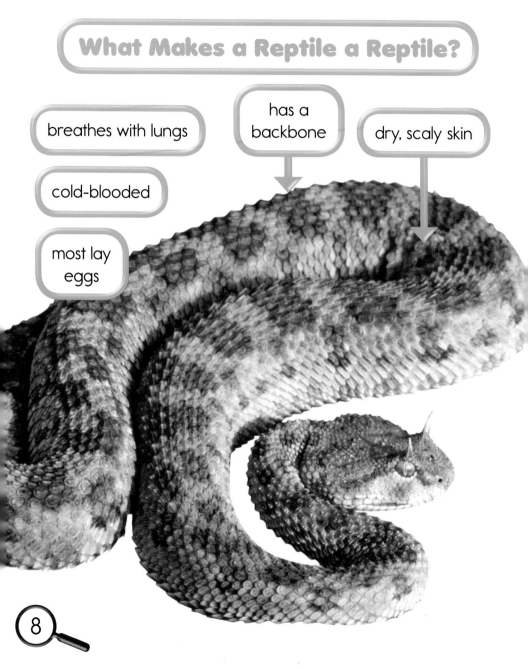

What Makes a Reptile a Reptile?

breathes with lungs

has a backbone

dry, scaly skin

cold-blooded

most lay eggs

There are four main kinds of reptiles. They are lizards, snakes, turtles, and the crocodile family. They all are covered in **scales**. They have other things in common, too. Take a look at the diagram to find out more.

The horned viper even has scales on its horns. The horns protect the snake's eyes from the bright sun.

Leaping Lizards

Chameleons (kuh-MEEL-yuns) are some of the strangest lizards. They are famous for changing color. They usually do this to show other chameleons how they feel.

Chameleons use their long, sticky tongues to catch insects. A chameleon's tongue is longer than the rest of its body!

Jackson's chameleon

FUN FACT!

Chameleons have cone-shaped eyes. They can look in two different directions at the same time!

Madagascar day gecko

leaf-tailed gecko

FUN FACT!

Geckos and other lizards have a special skill. If a predator grabs the lizard's tail, it breaks off. Then the lizard grows a new tail.

Geckos have superpowers! They can climb up walls and walk upside down on ceilings. Tiny hairs on their sticky toes help them cling to things.

Like most lizards, geckos want to hide. Some look like leaves, twigs, or bark. This **camouflage** helps them blend in with their surroundings.

The green basilisk lizard can run on water! It has special feet and a light body. It is superfast. That helps keep the lizard from sinking.

A green basilisk lizard darts across the water.

Tricky Turtles

Turtles are known for their shells. Shells protect their bodies. Some turtles have other tricks for staying safe. The stinkpot turtle can squirt a smelly odor. That sends enemies away.

The stinkpot is a tiny turtle with a big smell!

Other turtles have cool ways to catch food. The snake-necked turtle sticks out its long neck to grab **prey**.

A snapping turtle's tongue looks like a worm. A curious fish comes for a closer look. The turtle snatches it up.

FUN FACT!

Turtles are the only reptiles without teeth. They tear food with their sharp beaks.

snake-necked turtle

tongue

snapping turtle

19

vine snake

corn snake

gaboon viper

cobra

Sneaky Snakes

Many snakes have unusual
ways to hide and hunt.
The green vine snake sneaks
through trees. Corn snakes blend
in with the ground. The gaboon
viper kills prey with venom.
Spitting cobras can spray venom
up to eight feet (2.4 meters) away.

Like most reptiles, snakes eat meat. A few eat plants. But one snake is the pickiest eater! The African egg-eating snake eats only birds' eggs. It swallows the eggs whole.

FUN FACT!

Some snakes can go six months without eating.

The African egg-eating snake can swallow eggs twice the size of its head.

Gharials can make a
loud buzzing sound
with their snouts.

Killer Crocs

Crocodiles and alligators belong to a group called crocodilians. So does the odd-looking gharial (ger-EE-ahl). The gharial has a long, skinny snout and more than a hundred teeth. Its sharp teeth are perfect for catching fish.

There is no doubt about it. Reptiles really are remarkable!

Which Is Stranger?

desert horned lizard

- This lizard can shoot blood from its eyes! That scares away predators.

- It has long, pointed scales that look like spikes.

- If a predator is near, the desert horned lizard puffs up its body. It looks too big to eat!

You Decide!

flying dragon lizard

- The flying dragon lives in trees. It opens flaps of skin like wings to glide between the branches.

- It can steer through the air to land where it wants.

- Flying dragons only come to the ground to lay their eggs.

TOP 5 Facts
About Reptiles

 Dinosaurs were reptiles—really big reptiles, that is!

 Reptiles live on every continent except Antarctica. They often are found in warm places.

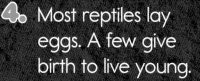 Most reptiles shed their skin. New skin grows underneath.

4. Most reptiles lay eggs. A few give birth to live young.

5. The marine iguana (ih-GWAH-nuh) is the only lizard that swims in the ocean. It also hunts there.

Record Holders

Biggest
The komodo dragon hunts deer and pigs.

Oldest
Giant tortoises can live more than 150 years.

Longest Snake
The reticulated python can grow as long as a bus.

Animal CRACK-UPS

Did this lizard just eat a blue lollipop? No! It is a blue-tongued skink. When a predator comes near, the skink puffs up. It hisses and sticks out its tongue. This frightens the predator into thinking the skink is dangerous.

JOKES

1. **What is a snake's favorite subject?**

2. **What is a turtle's favorite thing to wear?**

Answers: 1. HISS-tory! 2. A turtleneck sweater!

Glossary

camouflage (KAM-uh-flahzh): when an animal uses color, pattern, or shape to blend in with its surroundings

predator (PRED-uh-tur): animal that hunts other animals for food

prey (PRAY): animal that is hunted for food

scales (SKAYLS): small pieces of hard skin that cover the bodies of reptiles

Index

Facts for Now

Visit this Scholastic Web site for more information on reptiles:
www.factsfornow.scholastic.com
Enter the keyword **Reptiles**

About the Author

Lisa M. Herrington loves writing books about animals for kids. She lives in Connecticut with her husband, daughter, two fish, and no reptiles.